Little Rabbit

Retold by Diana Bentley

Illustrated by John Bendall-Brunello

Heinemann

Once upon a time
Little Rabbit saw a big carrot.
'I will go to my house
to eat the carrot,' she said.

Little Rabbit went home
but she could not get in.
Big Goat was in the house.

'Get out of my house!'
said Little Rabbit.
'No, no, no. I will not go,'
said Big Goat.

Little Rabbit went to find the cat.
'Big Goat is in my house,'
said Little Rabbit.
'Will you help?'

'No, no, no,' said the cat.
'Big Goat is too big.
I will not help you.'

Little Rabbit went to find the dog.
'Big Goat is in my house,'
said Little Rabbit.
'Will you help?'

'No, no, no,' said the dog.
'Big Goat is too big.
I will not help you.'

Buzzy Bee went to find Little Rabbit.
'I can help you,' she said.
'I can get Big Goat out.'

Buzzy Bee said to Big Goat,
'Will you go, go, go!'
Big Goat said,
'No, no, no. I will not go.'

'Oh yes, you will,' said Buzzy Bee.
'I can get you out.'
She went down the chimney.

'Ow! Ow! Ow!' said Big Goat,
and he ran out.
'Now I can eat my carrot,'
said Little Rabbit.